YOU LOST ACCESS

YOU LOST ACCESS

A Memoir of Boundaries, Power, and Becoming

ANGELA C. LE BLANC

For my son,
Travis G. Matthews

My firstborn son.

You were the first place my heart understood
what it meant to love without limit.

The world may close doors.
Time may change seasons.
Life may alter form.

But a mother never loses access to her child.

Not in memory.
Not in spirit.
Not in the quiet spaces where love still breathes.

Losing you did not end me.
It deepened me.
It refined my strength.
It taught me how to stand while carrying what cannot be set down.

Every boundary I built.
Every door I closed.
Every page I wrote.

Was shaped by loving you.

You are not behind me.
You are within me.

Always.

This becoming —
is for you.

— Mom

Access was never taken from me.

It was simply revealed who never deserved it.

AUTHOR'S NOTE

This is my story as I remember it.

It is written from lived experience, reflection, and truth as I understand it today. Some names, details, and timelines have been altered or combined, not to obscure meaning, but to protect privacy and honor boundaries.

This book is not written to accuse, defend, or justify. It is written to bear witness—to growth, to loss, to survival, and to becoming.

What follows is honest.

It is mine.

NOTE ON TRAUMA & HEALING

This book contains references to grief, illness, domestic violence, and survival.

Every experience shared within these pages reflects a lived moment. Some may feel familiar. Some may feel heavy.

Please move through this book at your own pace.

Pause when you need to.

Breathe when you need to.

Put it down when you need to.

Healing is not a race.

Strength is not measured by how much you can endure in silence.

If you are navigating your own loss, illness, or unsafe environment, consider seeking support from trusted professionals, community resources, or individuals trained to assist in times of crisis.

You are not weak for needing help.

You are human.

This memoir was written from a place of survival and from a place of becoming.

May you honor your own pace as you read.

DISCLAIMER

This memoir reflects the personal experiences and perspectives of the author.

All events are presented truthfully to the best of the author's recollection. Certain names, identifying details, and circumstances have been changed or omitted to protect the privacy of individuals.

The views expressed are solely those of the author and do not constitute legal, medical, psychological, or professional advice.

This book addresses sensitive topics including grief, illness, domestic violence, and personal loss. Readers are encouraged to seek qualified professional support if needed.

The author does not intend to defame, misrepresent, or cause harm to any individual or entity. Any resemblance to persons not directly identified is unintentional.

This work is protected by copyright. No portion may be reproduced, distributed, or transmitted in any form without written permission from the publisher.

Published by
Le Blanc Ventures LLC

SURVIVORSHIP NOTE

I am a breast cancer survivor.

That experience reshaped my understanding of time, strength, and presence. It is not the center of this story, but it is part of the woman who wrote it.

Table of Contents

CHAPTER ONE

The Shift

> *"Access rarely disappears overnight. It erodes before it ends."*

The shift did not arrive with chaos. There was no explosion. No betrayal dramatic enough to justify a clean exit. No singular event I could reference and say, That is when everything ended. If it had arrived that way, it would have been easier. Easier to explain. Easier to defend. Easier to close. But endings that begin with noise often leave room for negotiation. This one began in silence. At first, nothing was visibly wrong. I was still invited. Still included. Still present. But presence and belonging are not the same thing. I began noticing subtle changes. Not in what was said — but in what was felt. Conversations still happened, but they no longer landed the same way. Laughter still surfaced, but it felt thinner. My contributions were acknowledged, but not absorbed. There is a difference between being heard and being considered. I felt it first in my body. A tightening in my chest that did not belong to the day. A quiet fatigue that followed ordinary interactions. A heaviness that lingered after rooms emptied. Nothing had happened. And yet, something had shifted. That is the danger of quiet misalignment. It gives you no evidence. Only instinct.

At first, I dismissed it. I told myself I was overthinking. Overextended. Too sensitive. I rationalized. People evolve. Dynamics change. Energy fluctuates. I smoothed discomfort with logic before it could solidify into clarity. But discomfort, when ignored, accumulates. It gathers in moments so ordinary they almost escape notice. A delayed response where immediacy once existed. A glance that no longer searched for mine. A conversation that avoided depth without explanation. I began noticing how often I was the one adjusting. Softening tone. Reducing expectations. Translating my needs into something more digestible. I was recalibrating myself to preserve comfort. But comfort for whom? The realization did not come dramatically. It arrived one evening in a room that should have felt secure. Familiar faces. Familiar space. Familiar history. By every external measure, I belonged there. But as I sat listening, participating, offering presence, something became undeniable. I was no longer centered. Still included. But no longer anchored. Still welcomed. But no longer weighted. I had shifted from integral to optional. And optional is the beginning of erosion. There is a specific grief attached to that awareness. It does not demand tears. It demands honesty. You do not lose people all at once. You lose position first. You lose priority. You lose the unspoken assurance that your presence shapes the room. What disappears first is not the person. It is the illusion. The illusion that access is permanent. The illusion that proximity guarantees alignment. The illusion that history secures future relevance.

Once the illusion cracks, you begin observing differently. You begin measuring differently. You begin asking quiet questions: Who adjusts? Who absorbs? Who maintains? And most importantly — Who benefits? The shift was not about anger. It was about awareness. Awareness that I had been granting access automatically. Access to my time. Access to my energy. Access to my emotional labor. And access, when unexamined, becomes entitlement. That was the true beginning. Not the loss. The evaluation. The moment I stopped assuming access was mutual. The moment I started noticing the imbalance. The moment I realized something subtle but irreversible: I was being tolerated where I once belonged. And tolerance is not alignment. That is where the shift began. Not in chaos. In clarity. And once clarity enters the room, access is no longer guaranteed.

CHAPTER TWO

The Unraveling

> *"Awareness does not knock. It enters — and rearranges everything."*

Awareness doesn't arrive to comfort you. It arrives to disrupt. It does not ask if you're ready. It does not soften its delivery. It simply removes the filter. Once the shift revealed itself, I couldn't unsee it. Moments I would have brushed off before now lingered longer than they should. A tone. A pause. A hesitation disguised as thoughtfulness. Small inconsistencies grew louder. Not loud enough for accusation. But loud enough for intuition. This is how unraveling begins — not with confrontation, but with clarity that refuses to stay quiet. Nothing dramatic happened. No explosion. No betrayal with flashing lights. Just a quiet awareness that something wasn't balanced. Support appeared when it was convenient and disappeared when it required depth.

Encouragement was present in public but absent in private. Consistency showed up in words but faltered in action. The imbalance wasn't obvious. It was subtle. And subtlety is dangerous. Because subtlety teaches you to doubt yourself. It whispers, "Maybe you're overthinking." It suggests, "Maybe this is just adulthood." It convinces you that discomfort is maturity. So I adjusted. I edited my words before speaking. I softened needs before they could be dismissed. I reduced expectations before they could disappoint me. I translated my own feelings into something easier to digest. I called it compromise.

It wasn't. It was erosion. Erosion doesn't happen all at once. It happens gradually — grain by grain — until what was solid feels unfamiliar. I wasn't exhausted from doing too much. I was exhausted from carrying too much. Carrying the emotional temperature. Carrying the explanation. Carrying the hope that effort would eventually be reciprocated. I began shrinking in rooms where I once expanded. Laughing a little softer. Asking a little less. Needing a little less — at least outwardly. But internally, something was rising. The unraveling wasn't chaos. It was awareness collecting evidence.

Evidence that I had been compensating. Evidence that I had been over-functioning. Evidence that balance had been replaced with tolerance. And tolerance has a shelf life. There comes a moment when your spirit recognizes what your mouth has not yet admitted. That moment is quiet. But it is irreversible. I stopped defending what felt off. I stopped convincing myself that potential was progress. I stopped pretending that imbalance was normal. The unraveling didn't destroy me. It clarified me. It showed me where I had overextended. Where I had over-explained. Where I had over-accommodated. It revealed the places where I had mistaken endurance for strength. Strength does not require self-erasure. Maturity does not require self-minimization. Love does not require self-abandonment.

The unraveling wasn't an ending. It was a release. A release from pretending. A release from carrying both sides. A release from negotiating my own worth. What felt like falling apart was actually alignment. What felt like loss was actually clarity. And clarity does not apologize. The unraveling did not break me. It freed me.

Patterns

> *"What repeats is not a coincidence. It is permission."*

Patterns reveal themselves when emotion steps aside. Not during the argument. Not during the apology. Not in the middle of the confusion. They reveal themselves later — when the room is quiet and the replay begins. The same conversations. The same apologies. The same explanations delivered with different words but identical outcomes. Different tone. Same script. Different day. Same ending. At first, I called it growth in progress. I called it miscommunication. I called it timing. I called it everything except what it was. A cycle.

Patterns are subtle at the beginning. They disguise themselves as potential. As effort. As "we're working on it." But repetition leaves fingerprints. And once you notice them, you can't pretend you don't. Patterns don't lie. They repeat. What shook me wasn't the consistency in others. It was the consistency in myself. The pattern of over-explaining. The pattern of extending grace without evidence. The pattern of adjusting my boundaries to make someone else comfortable. I thought if I communicated better, the pattern would shift. If I was calmer, clearer, more patient — the outcome would finally change. It didn't. Because patterns don't respond to effort. They respond to access. And I was still granting it.

That was the quiet truth beneath everything. No one forced my participation. No one demanded my tolerance. I volunteered it. I allowed repeated behavior to feel temporary. I mistook familiarity for safety. And I confused potential with proof. Awareness is uncomfortable. It removes illusion. Once you see the pattern clearly, you lose the luxury of pretending it's accidental. The most painful realization was understanding that I was predictable. I would forgive. I would explain. I would stay. And patterns survive on predictability. So I stopped narrating my boundaries. I stopped warning about consequences. I stopped explaining what should already be understood. I didn't leave loudly. I didn't demand change. I shifted internally. That shift was everything. When I stopped participating, the rhythm broke. When I stopped reacting, the script collapsed. When I stopped granting access, the repetition lost its oxygen. Patterns don't break on their own. They only stop when you do. And when you stop — not emotionally, not impulsively — but decisively — you realize something powerful: The pattern was never stronger than you. It was just familiar.

Familiarity can feel like gravity. But gravity loses its pull when you step outside its field. That's when the pattern lost its power — not because it changed, but because I did. And when you change, what no longer aligns falls away without drama. Not everything that ends requires conflict. Some things dissolve the moment you withdraw permission. Patterns repeat. Until you don't.

CHAPTER FOUR

Silence Is a Discipline

"Not responding is a response. And it is often the strongest one."

Silence is not the absence of sound. It's the absence of reaction. It is the refusal to perform. The decision not to explain. The discipline of not correcting every misunderstanding. At first, silence felt like punishment. No notifications. No invitations. No noise to confirm I still existed in someone else's awareness. The world kept moving without checking whether I was watching. And that unsettled me. Because I had confused activity with relevance. Engagement with importance. Attention with value. That's when I learned how addicted I had been to response. Noise had always been proof. If something echoed back, it meant I mattered. If there was reaction, there was confirmation. If there was pursuit, there was validation. Silence stripped that illusion clean. It didn't argue. It didn't defend itself. It didn't rush to reassure me. It simply waited. And in that waiting, something uncomfortable surfaced — Who am I when no one is reacting to me? No applause. No pushback. No explanation requested. Just stillness.

Most people mistake silence for weakness. They assume nothing is happening. They assume you're retreating. They assume you're losing ground. They're wrong. Silence is strategy. It is where observation sharpens. Where clarity deepens. Where emotional discipline replaces impulse. In silence, you notice everything. Who reaches out only when they need something. Who disappears when there's nothing left to take. Who confuses proximity with loyalty. Who only values you when you're accessible. Without noise, patterns become undeniable. Silence removes distraction. It removes performance. It removes the illusion of urgency. And urgency is often manipulation in disguise. When you stop reacting immediately, you reclaim control of timing. When you stop answering every call to defend yourself, you reclaim authority over your narrative. When you stop proving your worth, you discover you never needed to. Silence taught me restraint. Restraint in speech. Restraint in explanation. Restraint in access. Not every accusation deserves correction. Not every misunderstanding deserves clarity. Not every departure deserves a response. Silence became my filter. It showed me who panicked when I was no longer predictable. It revealed who was comfortable only when I was accessible. It exposed who thrived on my availability. The loudest reactions often came from those who benefited most from my noise. Because silence removes leverage. When you are no longer reactive, you cannot be steered. When you are no longer explaining, you cannot be debated. When you are no longer defending, you cannot be exhausted.

Silence is not avoidance. It is containment. It is strength that does not need witnesses. Discipline isn't loud. It doesn't post about itself. It doesn't hint. It doesn't threaten. It holds. It waits. It observes. And in that observation, you learn who was aligned and who was simply nearby. Silence taught me that presence does not require performance. That worth does not require validation. That power does not require volume. The moment I stopped reacting, I stopped leaking energy. The moment I stopped explaining, I stopped negotiating my value. The moment I chose silence, I chose control. Silence is not passive. It is precision. And once you master it, you realize something profound — The loudest room belongs to the person who doesn't need to speak. Silence isn't emptiness. It's discipline. And discipline is freedom.

Withdrawal Looks Like Failure to People Who Need You Accessible

"When you stop being available, those who benefited will call it abandonment."

17

The first thing people notice when you withdraw isn't your absence. It's their inconvenience. They don't ask if you're okay. They ask why you changed. Why you're distant. Why you're quieter. Why you're no longer available on demand. The tone shifts quickly. Concern sounds like accusation. Curiosity sounds like interrogation. You become the problem for no longer solving theirs. They don't miss you. They miss access. There's a difference. Missing you is emotional. Missing access is practical. And practicality reveals motive.

I watched reactions shift the moment I stopped explaining myself. Silence made some people uncomfortable. Distance made others defensive. A few tried to bait me back into old roles. "Are you upset?" "You've changed." "You used to be different." Translation — You used to be easier to reach. Easier to influence. Easier to rely on without reciprocation. Others tried guilt. "I guess I just won't bother you anymore." "You think you're better now?" "Must be nice to have boundaries." Guilt is often the last tool when entitlement loses access.

And then there were the strategic gestures. Sudden kindness. Unexpected compliments. Selective nostalgia. Not reconciliation. Re-entry attempts. None of it was accidental. When you remove access, you expose expectation. When you enforce boundaries, you reveal who depended on your flexibility. Entitlement doesn't show itself when you are compliant. It shows itself when you are unavailable. I didn't announce my boundaries. I enforced them quietly. No speeches. No declarations. No dramatic exits. Just absence where there used to be immediacy. That unsettled people. Not because they valued me — but because they relied on me. My predictability had been currency. My compliance had been convenience. My willingness to absorb chaos had been infrastructure. I was the buffer. The mediator. The emotional shock absorber. And when I stepped back, systems malfunctioned. Confusion surfaced. Not because I was wrong. But because I was no longer cushioning impact. Withdrawal wasn't collapse. It was recalibration. Recalibration is quiet. It is the internal adjustment that restores balance. The version of me that was always reachable was expensive. She answered every call. Returned every message immediately. Made herself small to keep rooms calm. She carried emotional weight she did not create. She negotiated peace she did not disrupt. And she paid for it. With energy. With clarity. With time I will never recover. Accessibility had a cost. And I was the one funding it. This version — the one who pauses before responding, who evaluates before committing, who chooses before agreeing — costs less. Less stress. Less depletion. Less explanation. But demands more respect.

Respect unsettles those who benefited from your exhaustion. When you stop overextending, some will call you selfish. When you stop over-functioning, some will call you distant. When you stop over-giving, some will call you cold. Let them. Because what they are grieving is not you. They are grieving their access to you. Withdrawal looks like failure to people who relied on your availability. It looks like arrogance to people who depended on your humility. It looks like abandonment to people who never asked what it cost you to stay.

But withdrawal is not defeat. It is selection. Selection of where your energy goes. Selection of who earns proximity. Selection of what you tolerate. And selection is power. I did not disappear. I repositioned. And in that repositioning, I learned something unshakable — Access is not automatic. It is earned. And once revoked, it is not easily restored.

CHAPTER SIX

Control is Built, Not Claimed

"Control is not asserted. It is practiced."

Control doesn't arrive in a single decision. It is not something you wake up with because you are tired enough. It is not a personality trait you inherit. Control is built. It is constructed in repetition — in the moments no one applauds. It's choosing discipline on days when motivation disappears. It's holding your tongue when you could win the argument. It's declining invitations to chaos disguised as urgency. I used to think control meant dominance. Being the loudest voice. The most composed person in the room. The least visibly affected. That was a performance. Performance is exhausting because it depends on witnesses.

Real control is invisible. It's deciding not to respond when your ego wants the last word. It's walking away without creating a scene to justify your exit. It's allowing people to misunderstand you because clarification would only feed their narrative. Control is not controlling others. It is governing yourself. There were days I wanted to explain. Days I wanted to defend. Days I wanted to correct the story being told in rooms I no longer occupied. I didn't. Not because I was weak. Because I understood something finally — not every narrative needs your participation to survive. Some collapse on their own.

Control is walking away from the urge to manage perception. Control is refusing to manage everyone else's comfort. When I stopped reacting immediately, my world slowed down. When I stopped answering on demand, urgency dissolved. When I stopped performing strength, I started embodying it. Nothing dramatic happened. That's the point. Things stabilized. And stability is the most unglamorous form of power.

CHAPTER SEVEN

The Cost of Access

"If it costs you peace, it is not free."

Access feels generous. It feels kind. It feels inclusive. It feels mature. It feels like love. Until you calculate the cost. For a long time, I paid quietly. Not in dramatic sacrifices. Not in obvious depletion. In small withdrawals. Five minutes here. An emotional adjustment there. A conversation I didn't feel like having but agreed to anyway. An explanation offered before it was earned. The cost wasn't immediate. That's what made it dangerous.

I paid in time I didn't track. In emotional labor I never invoiced. In mental energy I dismissed because I was "strong enough" to handle it. Strength became my justification for overextension. If I could manage it, I did. If I could fix it, I tried. If I could smooth it over, I volunteered. Access became expectation. Availability became identity. If I responded quickly, I was dependable. If I accommodated, I was loyal. If I absorbed tension, I was mature. If I kept the peace, I was strong. No one asked whether I was tired. Because I never priced my accessibility. And when something is never priced, it is assumed to be free. Free advice. Free emotional regulation. Free conflict resolution. Free patience.

I normalized exhaustion as responsibility. I called it grace. But grace without boundaries becomes depletion. The real cost of access wasn't the time. It was the erosion. Erosion of focus. Erosion of clarity. Erosion of personal space. I would enter conversations already calculating how to prevent escalation. Already adjusting my tone to minimize discomfort. Already preparing to absorb whatever landed.

Access had turned me into infrastructure. Stable. Available. Load-bearing. And load-bearing structures crack quietly. The shift didn't begin with anger. It began with awareness. I noticed how quickly I responded to others and how slowly I responded to myself. How easily I prioritized urgency that wasn't mine. How often I overrode my own schedule for someone else's convenience. That's when I understood:

Access without boundaries is depletion disguised as virtue.

So I recalculated. Delayed responses became strategic. Selective engagement became necessary. Energy became currency. I stopped answering immediately. Stopped volunteering solutions. Stopped inserting myself into chaos that didn't originate with me. And suddenly, some people couldn't afford me. They called it distance. They called it ego. They called it change. They questioned my tone. My energy. My "availability." No one questioned the cost I had been absorbing. Because the system worked for them. Pricing access disrupts comfort.

When you start charging — not money, but standards — entitlement surfaces. People who were comfortable with unlimited entry begin negotiating. "Why are you different?" "You used to be so easy to talk to." "You're harder to reach now." Yes. Because I am no longer free. Not free in the sense of open access. Not free in the sense of unlimited availability. Not free in the sense of emotional on-call service. I am selective. And selection feels like rejection to people who relied on convenience. Access with no structure attracts dependence. Access with structure attracts respect. The ones who respected the adjustment stayed. They adapted to boundaries. They honored timing. They understood reciprocity. The ones who depended on my exhaustion left. Not because I pushed them away. Because the new terms required contribution. That was not loss. That was accounting.

When I finally calculated the cost, I realized something sobering: I had been overpaying for connections that underdelivered. Overextending for relationships that underinvested. Over-explaining for people committed to misunderstanding. Access without evaluation is emotional charity. And charity without limits breeds entitlement. Now access is intentional. It is earned. It is measured. It is reciprocal. I do not give immediate access to my time. I do not offer emotional labor without return. I do not allow familiarity to override respect. Access is not about isolation. It is about alignment. If it costs me peace, it is not free. If it drains clarity, it is not sustainable. If it requires self-negotiation, it is not alignment. The cost of access taught me value. And once you understand your value, you stop discounting it. Some people didn't lose access because I became cold. They lost access because I stopped subsidizing their comfort. That is not cruelty. That is correction. And correction is necessary when you finally understand what you have been paying for.

CHAPTER EIGHT

Grief Isn't Always Loud

"Not all endings scream. Some exhale."

Grief doesn't always arrive with tears. It doesn't always collapse your body onto the floor or announce itself with visible devastation. Sometimes it walks in quietly and rearranges the furniture of your expectations. Sometimes it looks like clarity. I didn't mourn people the way I thought I would. There were no dramatic goodbyes. No cinematic confrontations. No final conversations that wrapped everything neatly with understanding and apology. Most endings were quiet. Unacknowledged. Unspoken. Left suspended in unfinished sentences. At first, that unsettled me. I thought something was missing. I thought grief required ceremony. I thought closure was a prerequisite for peace. But grief doesn't require closure. It requires honesty. Honesty about what was real. Honesty about what was imagined. Honesty about how long you held something together that would not have survived on its own.

I didn't just grieve people. I grieved potential. I grieved the version of relationships that only existed because I kept them breathing. I grieved the effort I poured into maintaining connections that required constant intervention. I grieved the emotional CPR I performed on bonds that flatlined the moment I stopped trying. There is a specific kind of grief that comes from realizing you were the only one holding the weight. Not because the other person was evil. Not because there was always cruelty. But because reciprocity was never equal. I grieved the idea that some people would eventually meet me where I stood. That if I was patient enough, consistent enough, forgiving enough — alignment would arrive. It didn't. Grief forced me to acknowledge something uncomfortable: Some relationships survive on effort, not alignment. And when the effort stops, so do they. That realization stung. Because it meant I wasn't losing something stable. I was releasing something dependent.

There were no loud arguments to mark the end. No betrayals dramatic enough to justify anger. Just distance. Distance that grew without confrontation. Distance that felt confusing before it felt freeing. Grief isn't always loud. Sometimes it is the quiet acceptance that something has already ended, even if you are still technically connected. I grieved the time invested. The energy extended. The parts of myself that adjusted in order to sustain what was fragile. I grieved the version of me who believed endurance would be rewarded. And then something unexpected followed. Relief. Not immediate. Not triumphant. Subtle. Like setting down something heavy you forgot you were carrying. Relief that I no longer had to maintain it. Relief that I no longer had to strategize around it. Relief that I no longer had to anticipate the imbalance.

Grief cleared space. It removed the background noise I had mistaken for companionship. It revealed how often I had confused activity with connection. Silence replaced tension. And silence felt lighter. Longing shifted into acceptance. Not the soft acceptance that hopes for reconciliation. The final kind. The kind that doesn't circle back. The kind that doesn't rehearse alternate endings. Some people were never meant to walk the next stretch of road with me. They were meant to accompany me until I stopped shrinking.

They were meant to exist in chapters where I was still negotiating my worth. When I stopped negotiating, the alignment shifted. That wasn't cruelty. It wasn't abandonment. It was evolution.

Grief is often misunderstood as weakness. But grief is evidence that you cared. It is the recognition that something mattered — even if it wasn't sustainable. I didn't leave with bitterness. I left with awareness. Awareness that not every connection is meant to mature. Some are meant to instruct. Some are meant to mirror. Some are meant to end the moment you stop over-functioning. Grief taught me that endings do not require spectacle to be valid. They do not require consensus to be real. They do not require both parties to agree that it is over. Sometimes grief is simply the quiet understanding that what once fit no longer aligns. And alignment is not negotiable. When I stopped explaining, some relationships ended. Not because I attacked them. But because they depended on explanation to survive. Grief didn't hollow me. It refined me. It showed me what was mutual. And what was maintenance. It showed me which connections breathed on their own. And which required constant resuscitation. Grief made room. And room is necessary for growth.

There is a sacredness in allowing something to end without dragging it through ceremony. No performance. No spectacle. Just acceptance. Some people were never meant to come with me. They were meant to end where I stopped explaining. That wasn't cold. It was honest. And honesty is a form of alignment.

CHAPTER NINE

Boundaries Are Not Invitations

> *"A boundary explained too many times becomes optional."*

Boundaries are often misunderstood as requests. They are not. They are not suggestions. They are not warnings. They are not emotional outbursts disguised as self-protection. A boundary is a decision. It does not ask for agreement. It does not seek validation. It does not require applause. It simply defines what will happen next. For a long time, I confused boundaries with conversations. I thought if I explained myself clearly enough, patiently enough, calmly enough, people would adjust. They didn't. Because explanation invites interpretation. Interpretation invites negotiation. Negotiation invites erosion. And erosion is subtle. The more you justify a boundary, the more it sounds flexible. The more flexible it sounds, the less real it becomes. So I stopped announcing mine. Announcements invite debate. Enforcement does not. The shift wasn't loud. There were no declarations. No dramatic speeches about self-respect. No ultimatums delivered with shaking hands. Just structural changes. Fewer responses. Shorter answers. Less access. More space.

When boundaries are real, people feel them before they hear them. Tone shifts. Energy changes. Expectations recalibrate. Or they resist. Resistance is information. The most revealing moments came quietly. A message sent late, expecting immediate response. A favor requested without warning, assuming compliance. An expectation slipped casually into conversation, hoping I wouldn't notice. I noticed everything. But I didn't react emotionally. Reaction feeds negotiation. I responded structurally. Access reduced. Distance applied. Availability adjusted. No explanation issued. That is the part most people struggle with. They want dialogue. They want debate. They want you to defend the line. But a real boundary does not defend itself. It functions. If someone crosses it, there is consequence. Not anger. Not drama. Not punishment. Consequence. Energy shifts. Access changes. Engagement narrows. Boundaries are not about controlling others. They are about controlling proximity. Who gets close. Who stays close. Who no longer qualifies. For years, I thought boundaries would make me difficult. Cold. Unapproachable. Unkind. What they actually made me was stable. I stopped over-explaining. Stopped absorbing discomfort that wasn't mine. Stopped tolerating behavior simply because I could endure it. Endurance is not the same as acceptance. Tolerance is not the same as agreement. Boundaries clarified what I valued. Time. Energy. Respect. Reciprocity. And once clarified, I protected them.

There is discomfort in enforcing boundaries. Not because they are wrong. Because they reveal entitlement. When someone benefits from your flexibility, your firmness feels personal. When someone relies on your over-accommodation, your consistency feels hostile. But hostility is not the goal. Alignment is. Some people adjusted. They respected timing. They honored space. They recalibrated their expectations. Others left. Both outcomes were useful. Boundaries filter. They filter intention. They filter entitlement. They filter dependency disguised as closeness. Consistency is what makes them real.

If today you enforce and tomorrow you retract, the line dissolves. Consistency doesn't argue. It repeats. It holds. It does not escalate. It does not chase. It does not over-clarify. It simply remains. Boundaries are not walls. They are gates. Walls keep everyone out. Gates allow entry — selectively. The difference is intention. When I stopped inviting debate, peace increased. When I stopped explaining myself twice, exhaustion decreased. When I stopped reacting emotionally, power stabilized. Boundaries are not about isolation. They are about structure. Structure prevents chaos. Structure prevents erosion. Structure protects alignment. And once I understood that, something shifted permanently. I no longer feared being misunderstood. I feared being misaligned. Boundaries did not make me rigid. They made me deliberate. And deliberate is dangerous to those who relied on your flexibility. But deliberate is safe for you. Boundaries don't require confrontation. They require consistency. And consistency doesn't argue. It stands.

CHAPTER TEN

You Don't Get Closure, You Get Distance

"Distance ends what dialogue prolongs."

Closure is a myth people cling to when they want an ending that doesn't hurt. It sounds mature. It sounds evolved. It sounds like something emotionally intelligent people pursue. But most of the time, closure is just a softer word for one more conversation. One more explanation. One more chance to be understood. One more attempt to make the ending feel mutual. Real endings don't work like that. They don't gather everyone at the table for final remarks. They don't tie loose threads into bows. They don't offer a speech that makes both sides feel seen.

Real endings create distance. Clean. Unapologetic. Unreversed.

For a long time, I waited for closure. Waited for acknowledgment. Waited for understanding. Waited for someone to say, "I see what happened." Waiting felt noble. It wasn't. Waiting implied permission. Waiting suggested someone else had authority over how things concluded. They didn't. The moment I realized that, something shifted. Closure assumes shared accountability. Distance assumes personal responsibility. I stopped waiting for someone else to validate my exit. Stopped rehearsing final conversations in my head. Stopped imagining the perfect articulation of why this no longer worked. Because the truth is — if someone truly needed an explanation to understand your departure, they likely ignored the signs that led to it. Distance did what explanations never could. It ended loops. Loops of rehashing. Loops of revisiting. Loops of revising history to soften accountability. Distance shut down arguments that hadn't even been spoken yet. It removed the temptation to return out of nostalgia. Nostalgia is deceptive. It edits memory. It softens impact. It romanticizes what exhausted you. Distance prevents that distortion. Without access, there is no revision. Without proximity, there is no reinterpretation. Without conversation, there is no reopening.

Some people called it cold. Others called it avoidance. But those labels revealed more about their discomfort than my decision. Cold implies lack of feeling. I felt everything. Avoidance implies fear. I was clear. The distance wasn't emotional. It was logistical. It simplified my life in ways no conversation ever had. Fewer variables. Fewer interruptions. Fewer emotional negotiations. Distance removed the constant recalibration I had grown used to. It eliminated the need to explain tone. To defend decisions. To justify boundaries. Closure asks you to relive what already proved unworkable. It invites you back into the dynamic for one more round. Distance refuses the invitation. Distance says, "The decision has already been made." And that is what made it powerful.

When you choose distance, you stop trying to manage how others process your departure. You stop softening the ending to protect someone else's comfort. You stop diluting the truth to avoid being misunderstood. Distance does not argue. It does not persuade. It does not circle back. It creates space wide enough that repetition becomes impossible. And repetition is what kept everything alive longer than it should have been. There was a quiet strength in no longer seeking agreement. In no longer explaining the obvious. In no longer defending the decision to leave something that required constant defense. Distance is not cruelty. It is clarity applied. It is the recognition that resolution does not require participation. It requires removal. The absence of dialogue does not mean the absence of thought. It means the presence of certainty.

I did not choose distance because I lacked emotion. I chose it because emotion had already been exhausted. I chose it because explanation had already been attempted. I chose it because clarity had already arrived. Closure seeks to soothe. Distance seeks to protect. And protection is not selfish. It is necessary. I stopped waiting for someone else to close the door. I closed it. Not loudly. Not dramatically. But completely. Because some endings do not need conversation. They need space. And space is what prevents return. I did not get closure. I got distance. And the distance was enough.

CHAPTER ELEVEN

Discipline Is Lonelier Than Chaos

> *"Chaos keeps you surrounded. Discipline teaches you to stand."*

Chaos is crowded. There is always something happening. Someone reacting. Someone responding. Someone explaining. Chaos creates roles. The fixer. The mediator. The one who absorbs. The one who stays too long. In chaos, you are never without relevance. There is always a problem to solve. A tension to manage. A fire to extinguish. And that feels important. It feels necessary. It feels alive. Discipline does not feel like that. Discipline is quiet. It does not gather an audience. It does not reward you with immediate validation. It does not create urgency that makes you feel essential. It is repetitive. Wake up. Follow through. Hold the line. Repeat. No applause. No spectacle. No emotional intensity to prove that something is shifting.

At first, that quiet felt unfamiliar. Unsettling. There were moments when I missed the urgency of chaos. Not because it was healthy. Because it was stimulating. Chaos produces adrenaline. Adrenaline mimics purpose. When everything feels urgent, you feel needed. When something is always unfolding, you feel involved. Discipline removes urgency. It replaces it with structure. Structure feels slower. Less dramatic. Less visible. And that invisibility can feel lonely. Chaos rarely leaves you alone with yourself. Discipline does. In the quiet, there are no distractions. No external emergencies to manage. No emotional storms to navigate. Just you. And your habits. That was uncomfortable. Because chaos had allowed me to hide. Hide behind busyness. Hide behind reaction. Hide behind the constant need to respond. Discipline exposed everything. The impulse to check. The urge to respond immediately. The reflex to over-function. Without chaos to mask it, I could see how much of my identity had been built around being necessary. Necessary feels powerful. Disciplined feels independent. Independence reduces noise. And noise had been familiar.

There were days when discipline felt anticlimactic. No breakthrough moment. No dramatic shift. Just consistency. Consistency is humbling. It demands the same effort when no one is observing. It requires the same standards when no one is challenging them. It asks you to hold boundaries even when they are not being tested. That's where loneliness lives. Not in isolation. In repetition. You show up the same way when there is no crisis forcing you to. You choose restraint when reaction would feel satisfying. You stay aligned when misalignment would be easier. Chaos had kept me externally focused. Discipline forced internal accountability. It asked questions chaos never did: Who are you when nothing is happening? Who are you when no one needs you? Who are you when silence replaces urgency? That is a confronting place to stand. Because without crisis, there is no excuse. Without disruption, there is no distraction. Without chaos, there is only structure. And structure requires ownership. But discipline gave me something chaos never could. Stability without exhaustion.

In chaos, stability is temporary. It is achieved through overexertion. In discipline, stability compounds. You are not constantly recalibrating. You are not constantly recovering. You are not constantly anticipating the next shift. You are steady. Steady can feel boring at first. But boring is peaceful. Peaceful is sustainable. Sustainable is powerful. Lonely does not mean wrong. Quiet does not mean empty. It means there is no performance required. It means you are no longer fueled by reaction. It means you are building something that does not depend on spectacle. Discipline rewires the nervous system. It teaches you that calm is not absence. Calm is safety. It teaches you that growth does not have to feel dramatic to be real. It teaches you that repetition is not stagnation. It is reinforcement. Chaos attracts attention. Discipline attracts results. Chaos keeps you surrounded. Discipline teaches you to stand alone without feeling abandoned. And once you can stand alone without needing noise to validate you, you are no longer vulnerable to chaos. You are stable. You are intentional. You are building. And what you build in quiet does not collapse in noise.

CHAPTER TWELVE

This Is Where Access Ends

> *"Access ends quietly. Permanence does not require volume."*

Access doesn't end with an announcement. There is no press release. No final warning. No dramatic speech declaring the shift. Access ends with a decision that doesn't reverse. And reversal is the detail that matters. For a long time, my exits were conditional. Temporary distance. Emotional pauses. Boundaries delivered with the possibility of negotiation. This was different. There was no single explosive moment that marked the shift. No betrayal dramatic enough to justify a scene. No confrontation that made the ending obvious to everyone involved.

Just accumulation. A series of small, deliberate choices that added up to something permanent.

I stopped re-entering spaces that required me to shrink. Stopped volunteering clarity where confusion was intentional. Stopped responding to dynamics that depended on my tolerance. Tolerance is often mislabeled as strength. It isn't. It is capacity without correction. And I had too much capacity. I mistook familiarity for safety. Just because something is known does not mean it is secure. Just because something is predictable does not mean it is aligned. That distinction changed everything. Access narrowed. Not dramatically. Gradually. Response time shifted. Availability recalibrated. Proximity adjusted. Not everyone noticed immediately. Some assumed it was stress. Others assumed it was temporary. A phase. They expected elasticity. They were used to elasticity. They were used to my flexibility bending back into place. But this time, it did not bend. Because this time, it was not reactive. It was structural.

Access had become intentional. Measured. Conditional in ways it had never been before. Not as punishment. As protection. Protection of time. Protection of energy. Protection of the self I was building. When access is public, everyone feels entitled to it. When access becomes private, entitlement reveals itself. The shift unsettled some people. Not because they valued me deeply. Because they relied on my predictability. Predictability is comforting. You know who will answer. You know who will show up. You know who will absorb impact. When that predictability disappears, discomfort surfaces. I did not argue about it. I did not clarify it. I simply remained consistent. Consistency is what makes a boundary permanent. If today you retract and tomorrow you enforce, access remains negotiable. If you enforce without commentary, access recalibrates. What remained were relationships that didn't require constant maintenance. Conversations that did not drain me. Silence that felt aligned instead of heavy. There is a difference between loneliness and relief.

Before, silence felt like absence. Now it felt like space. Space to think. Space to plan. Space to breathe without managing someone else's emotional temperature. That is when I knew the shift was complete. When I no longer felt the urge to re-enter. When nostalgia no longer tempted me. When explanation no longer felt necessary. Completion is quiet. It does not seek validation. It does not require agreement. It simply remains unchanged. Access did not disappear. It just stopped being public. It stopped being assumed. It stopped being unlimited. Access became earned. Selective. Aligned. Some people interpreted that as distance. Others interpreted it as transformation. Both were correct. Because when you change your standards, you change your proximity. And proximity is power. Access ended not because I was angry. Not because I was hurt. Not because I wanted control.

Access ended because the version of me that tolerated misalignment no longer existed. There was no dramatic door slam. Just a door that no longer opened. And the quiet of that permanence was louder than any confrontation. This is where access ends. Not with spectacle. With structure. Not with emotion. With alignment. Not with explanation. With decision. And decisions that do not reverse are the ones that reshape your life.

CHAPTER THIRTEEN

Stability Isn't Exciting, It's Effective

> *"Excitement fluctuates. Stability compounds."*

Stability doesn't announce itself. It doesn't arrive with applause. It doesn't post a victory update. It doesn't signal arrival with fireworks. It just works. At first, I didn't recognize it. I was conditioned to measure progress by intensity. By emotional swings. By urgent decisions. By visible reactions that proved something significant was happening. Growth, in my mind, had always felt dramatic. A breakthrough. A confrontation. A bold exit. Stability felt... anticlimactic. No highs. No crashes. No emotional whiplash. Just forward movement. Quiet days that did not require survival. Evenings that did not require recovery. Mornings that did not require repair. That felt unfamiliar.

For so long, I had equated peace with stagnation. If nothing was happening, I assumed nothing was changing. But stability is not stagnation. It is alignment maintained. Days stopped feeling like obstacles to survive and started feeling like structures I could rely on. Routines replaced recovery. Planning replaced reaction. Consistency replaced adrenaline. And that shift changed everything. When your nervous system is used to chaos, calm feels suspicious. You look for disruption. You anticipate interruption. You brace for impact that never arrives. It takes time to trust stability. Because stability requires you to sit still long enough to realize the storm is not coming. Stability doesn't stimulate. It sustains. It removes volatility. It eliminates emotional emergencies. It reduces unpredictability. And when unpredictability disappears, something else happens. Excuses disappear with it. That's when I understood why so many people avoid stability. Stability removes narrative. There's no dramatic villain. No ongoing crisis. No chaos to point at as justification. When things are steady, there is nowhere to hide unfinished business. No instability to blame for inconsistency. No emotional turbulence to excuse poor discipline.

Stability demands accountability. If the structure is solid, the only variable left is you. That can be confronting. Because once chaos is gone, your habits become visible. Your follow-through becomes measurable. Your discipline becomes undeniable. Stability exposes what you build when no one is disrupting you. It reveals whether you were truly growing — or merely surviving. For years, I had mastered survival. Adaptation. Tolerance. Emotional navigation. But survival is reactive. Stability is proactive. In survival mode, you respond to circumstances. In stability, you create them. You decide the pace. You decide the structure. You decide the boundaries. Stability gave me space. Space to plan beyond the week. Space to think beyond the moment. Space to build beyond repair. There is something powerful about waking up and not needing to fix anything. No emotional debris. No unresolved tension. No urgent recalibration. Just rhythm. And rhythm compounds. Small habits repeated without interruption. Small decisions that align without correction. Small progress that accumulates without collapse. Stability doesn't feel impressive in real time. But its impact is exponential.

I realized how much effort chaos required. How much energy went into maintaining volatility. How much emotional labor was spent managing disruption. Stability costs less. And delivers more. It is not thrilling. It is effective. Effective builds legacy. Thrilling builds stories. I chose legacy. Once I understood that stability was not boredom but momentum, I stopped craving intensity. I stopped needing dramatic proof that growth was happening. Growth was happening in the quiet. In the routine. In the consistency that did not require recovery. There is freedom in not being constantly tested. There is strength in not being constantly triggered. There is power in building without interruption. Stability does not shout. It structures. It does not perform. It produces. And when production replaces performance, peace becomes sustainable. I didn't miss the chaos once I calculated its cost. I didn't romanticize instability once I experienced rhythm. I didn't crave disruption once I trusted structure. Stability isn't exciting. It doesn't need to be. It works. And what works consistently outlasts what entertains temporarily.

CHAPTER FOURTEEN

Not Everything Needs to Be Reclaimed

"Completion is not loss. It is accuracy."

There is a narrative people love. Reclaim everything. Take back what was lost. Recover every piece of yourself that slipped away. It sounds powerful. It sounds triumphant. It sounds like strength. But not everything needs to be reclaimed. Some things are not lost. They are completed. For a long time, I believed growth meant retrieval. That if I healed enough, matured enough, clarified enough — I would return to reclaim what once felt important. Old relationships. Old dynamics. Old versions of myself.

But healing is not a scavenger hunt. It is discernment. Discernment requires you to ask a harder question: Does this still fit? Not, Did it once matter? Not, Did I invest in it? Not, Could it work now if I try harder? Does it fit who I am now? Growth changes scale. What once felt expansive may now feel constricting. What once felt necessary may now feel heavy. What once felt aligned may now feel miscalculated. Reclamation assumes something was taken from you. Sometimes nothing was taken. Sometimes you simply outgrew it. I stopped romanticizing the past. Stopped revisiting old rooms just to prove I had changed. Stopped chasing dynamics that only felt meaningful because they were familiar. Familiarity is powerful. It whispers comfort. It offers memory. It tempts you with nostalgia. But nostalgia edits reality. It softens edges. It erases imbalance. It remembers effort and forgets erosion.

I realized something sobering: Some versions of me only existed because I was surviving something. They were adaptive. They were necessary. They were strong. But they were temporary. Survival identities are not meant to be permanent residences. They are bridges. And bridges are meant to be crossed — not lived on. Reclamation sounds bold. But sometimes release is braver. It takes discipline to leave something unfinished on purpose. To accept that not every conversation will be resolved. Not every misunderstanding will be corrected. Not every narrative will be rewritten. Completion does not require consensus. It requires clarity. I stopped trying to reclaim relationships that required my over-functioning. Stopped trying to reclaim conversations that depended on explanation. Stopped trying to reclaim proximity that relied on my elasticity. If it only worked when I shrank, it does not belong in my expansion. There is power in letting something expire without forcing revival. Not because it failed. Because its purpose was fulfilled.

Some connections were teachers. Some were mirrors. Some were momentum. They were not destinations. Growth is not about accumulating. It is about refining. Refinement means subtraction. It means acknowledging that what once supported you may now slow you. It means releasing identities that were built around struggle. I no longer need to reclaim who I was when I tolerated misalignment. I do not need to retrieve the version of me who absorbed imbalance. I do not need to revisit dynamics that only thrived in chaos. That is not regression. That is accuracy. Accuracy requires courage. It requires you to stop proving loyalty to things that no longer fit. It requires you to accept that some chapters were temporary by design. Not everything that mattered must continue. Not everything that shaped you must follow you. Not everything that once felt like home is meant to remain familiar. I kept what aligned. I discarded what didn't. Without ceremony. Without bitterness. Without drama. Nothing was wasted. Every experience refined my standards. Every misalignment clarified my boundaries. Every ending strengthened my discernment.

Reclamation is powerful when something was unjustly taken. But when something simply expired, restoration is unnecessary. You do not rebuild a bridge you have already crossed. You do not reclaim a season that has already served its purpose. You move forward. Whole. Not because you retrieved everything. Because you released what no longer fits. Completion is not weakness. It is precision. And precision is how you build a life that no longer requires rescue.

CHAPTER FIFTEEN

Power Looks Different When You're Not Performing

> *"Power that needs witnesses is performance.*
> *Power that stands alone is freedom."*

57

Power used to feel like visibility. Being noticed. Being needed. Being acknowledged. There was a time when I measured strength by reaction. If people responded, I felt effective. If people adjusted, I felt influential. If people reacted emotionally, I felt powerful. That version of power was loud. It required audience. It required resistance. It required proof. But performance is exhausting. Because when power depends on reaction, you are still tethered to response. Still watching the room. Still monitoring the impact.

Still calibrating tone for effect. That is not power. That is management. Real power is quieter. It does not need immediate acknowledgment. It does not shift when attention moves elsewhere. It does not panic when misunderstood. It simply exists. There is a difference between being seen as powerful and being powerful. Being seen requires effort. Being powerful requires alignment.

When I stopped performing strength, something changed. I no longer needed to correct narratives. I no longer needed to prove growth. I no longer needed to demonstrate detachment. Detachment demonstrated itself. Silence became enough. Consistency became proof. Distance became confirmation. Power is knowing you can walk away — and not waiting to be chased. It is not announcing your standards. It is living by them. It is not demanding respect. It is behaving in ways that make disrespect expensive. There was a time when I believed power meant control. Control of perception. Control of narrative. Control of how I was received. But the need to control perception is insecurity disguised as confidence. When you are grounded, perception loses leverage. Let them misunderstand. Let them speculate. Let them construct versions of you that fit their comfort.

Your reality does not bend to their interpretation. Power is emotional independence. Not indifference.

Indifference is cold. Independence is steady. I no longer require validation to feel secure in my decisions. I no longer require applause to maintain my discipline. I no longer require confrontation to confirm my boundaries. What once felt like proving now feels like preserving. Preserving energy. Preserving peace. Preserving direction. Power looks different when you are not performing. It looks less dramatic. Less reactive. Less visible. But more stable. It does not fluctuate with approval. It does not collapse under criticism. It does not overextend to maintain relevance. When I stopped performing, I stopped exhausting myself trying to be understood. I stopped explaining my evolution. I stopped softening my growth to keep others comfortable. Comfort is not my responsibility. Alignment is. There is strength in not responding. Strength in not reacting. Strength in not re-entering. But the deepest strength is in not caring whether someone sees it. Power without witnesses is freedom. Freedom from emotional dependency. Freedom from narrative management. Freedom from proving your worth through performance.

I used to think power required presence. Now I understand it requires position. Position in your standards. Position in your boundaries. Position in your clarity. When you are positioned correctly, you do not chase. You are not convinced. You do not overexplain. You stand. And standing quietly is more powerful than shouting loudly. Performance fades. Alignment compounds. Visibility fluctuates. Integrity remains. This is what power looks like when you are no longer performing. It is calm. It is deliberate. It is selective. It is unmoved. It does not need to be announced. It is understood — by the only person whose understanding matters. Me.

CHAPTER SIXTEEN

Peace Isn't Passive

"Peace is not the absence of conflict. It is the refusal to participate in it."

Peace has a reputation for being soft. Gentle. Yielding. Quiet in a way that suggests surrender. That version of peace is incomplete. Real peace is deliberate. It is chosen. It is enforced. It does not arrive because everything around you becomes calm. It arrives because you stop engaging with what destabilizes you. I did not find peace by fixing everyone. I did not find it by resolving every misunderstanding. I did not find it by being understood. I found it by refusing to keep reopening doors that led nowhere. Refusing to rehearse conversations that would never be productive.

Refusing to prepare defenses for battles that only existed if I stayed available. Peace required restraint. Restraint from responding immediately. Restraint from correcting narratives. Restraint from explaining myself twice. Restraint from re-entering rooms where my energy would be negotiated. Peace is not passive. It is active discipline. It is the strength to say no internally before you ever say it aloud. It is the ability to sit in silence without filling it with justification. It is the refusal to let urgency override clarity.

For a long time, I believed peace would feel euphoric. Light. Expansive. Effortless. Instead, it felt structured. Measured. Intentional. Peace required boundaries that did not bend when tested. It required consistency when nostalgia tempted me. It required trust in my own judgment — even when no one validated it. Especially then. Peace forced me to confront how addicted I had been to resolution. How often I equated "fixing it" with maturity. How often I believed harmony required participation. But not all conflict deserves resolution. Some deserve removal. Peace is knowing when engagement is optional. Peace is understanding that not every misunderstanding requires correction. Peace is accepting that some narratives will exist without your input. And being unbothered by it. That unbothered state does not mean numbness. It means stability. Stability without hyper-vigilance. Without bracing for disruption. Without anticipating the next emotional shift. Peace recalibrated my nervous system. Where there was once tension, there is now pause. Where there was once reaction, there is now assessment. Where there was once urgency, there is now choice. Choice is powerful. When you realize you are not obligated to respond, you begin to conserve energy. When you realize you are not obligated to explain, you begin to protect clarity. When you realize you are not obligated to participate, you begin to reclaim control. Peace reduces noise. Reduced proximity. Reduced unnecessary access. It made my life simpler. Fewer variables. Fewer interruptions. Fewer emotional negotiations. Peace is selective. It chooses where energy flows. It chooses what enters. It chooses what remains outside. It does not attempt to control everything. It controls participation. That distinction changed everything.

Peace does not mean I am unaffected. It means I am unmoved. Unmoved by tactics. Unmoved by pressure. Unmoved by expectation. Peace is not retreat. It is positioning. Positioning myself where my energy is not constantly tested. Where my boundaries are not constantly negotiated. Where my identity is not constantly defended. Peace is expensive. It costs ego. It costs the desire to win. It costs the satisfaction of being right. It costs the performance of strength.

But what it gives back is priceless. Clarity. Stability. Sustainability. There is power in knowing you can engage — and choosing not to. Power in knowing you can argue — and choosing silence. Power in knowing you can re-enter — and choosing distance. Peace is not the absence of chaos. It is the mastery of self within it. And once mastered, chaos loses its appeal. Because chaos demands reaction. Peace demands alignment. Alignment does not shout. It holds. It protects. It sustains. Peace isn't passive. It is disciplined. And discipline is what keeps it intact.

CHAPTER SEVENTEEN

The Version of Me That Stayed Didn't Survive

> *"Survival was necessary. It was never meant to be permanent."*

65

People talk about survival as if it is the goal. It isn't. Survival is a response. It is the version of you that adapts quickly, tolerates deeply, and endures silently. It is alert. It is vigilant. It is prepared for disruption. The version of me that stayed survived. She absorbed. She adjusted. She negotiated. She endured. She knew how to keep the peace. How to soften the tone. How to remain present even when presence required self-erasure.

She survived environments that demanded flexibility without reciprocity. She maintained connections that relied on her endurance. She stood firm in places that did not return the same stability. And for a time, that was strength. But survival is not sustainable. The version of me that stayed lived in constant readiness. Ready to explain. Ready to fix. Ready to recalibrate the emotional temperature of a room. She confused endurance with maturity. She confused patience with progress. She believed loyalty meant remaining, even when remaining required shrinking. That version of me was not weak. She was strategic. She did what she needed to do to navigate what was in front of her. But she was not meant to last forever. There comes a moment when survival becomes stagnation. When endurance becomes self-abandonment. When staying becomes self-betrayal. I did not resent the version of me who stayed. I thanked her. She protected me when I needed protection. She tolerated when I lacked clarity. She endured while I was still learning. But she does not represent who I am now. Growth required her retirement. Not because she failed. Because she completed her assignment.

Survival identities are temporary structures. They help you cross difficult terrain. They are not meant to become permanent architecture. The version of me that stands now does not stay where she is diminished.

She does not negotiate her worth. She does not confuse familiarity with safety. She does not accept imbalance as inevitability. She evaluates. She selects. She moves deliberately. She understands that peace is not maintained by endurance but by alignment. There was grief in releasing the old version of myself. Not because I wanted to return to her. But because she carried so much.

She was strong in ways that were invisible. Strong in silence. Strong in restraint. Strong in composure. But she carried more than she should have. The new version carries less. Less tension. Less urgency. Less responsibility for what does not belong to her. The old version survived. The new version lives. That is the difference. Living does not require constant defense. It does not require constant vigilance. It does not require constant recalibration. Living requires clarity. Clarity about what aligns. Clarity about what fits. Clarity about what remains and what ends. The version of me that stayed did not survive this transformation. She was replaced. Not by someone colder. Not by someone harsher. By someone clearer. Clearer about boundaries. Clearer about standards. Clearer about the cost of remaining in places that require shrinking.

Survival was once necessary. It is no longer my identity. I am no longer the one who stays past expiration. I am no longer the one who absorbs imbalance as proof of strength. I am no longer the one who equates endurance with love. That version did not survive. She was honored. And then she was released. What remains is deliberate. Stable. Aligned. And unwilling to shrink.

CHAPTER EIGHTEEN

You Lost Access

> *"Access was never permanent. It was conditional on alignment."*

This was never about punishment. Not ego. Not pride. Not revenge disguised as growth. This was about conclusion. People mistake access for ownership. They assume that once proximity is granted, it becomes permanent. That history secures position. That familiarity guarantees entry. It doesn't. Access is a privilege. And privileges expire when alignment does. There was no dramatic rupture. No explosion loud enough to justify a spectacle. By the time access ended, the emotion had already burned off.

What remained was clarity. Clarity is quiet. It does not beg. It does not debate. It does not revisit. I did not revoke access loudly. I did not post about it. I did not announce it in coded language. I did not gather witnesses to validate the shift. I adjusted proximity. And I never adjusted it back. That is what made it final. Some assumed it was temporary. They expected elasticity. They expected the version of me who always reconsidered. Who always reopened doors after cooling off. Who always translated boundaries into something softer. That version no longer existed. Access ended because tolerance expired. Because discipline stabilized. Because boundaries held. Because distance worked.

You didn't lose access because I changed moods. You lost access because I changed standards. There is a difference. Moods fluctuate. Standards solidify. When standards rise, access narrows. Not everyone qualifies for the next version of you. Qualification is not personal. It is structural. Access is proximity to energy. To time. To thought. To emotional investment. To influence. When access is unlimited, your energy is diluted. When access is selective, your energy compounds. I stopped diluting. That is what felt like loss. Not because I became cold. Because I became clear. Clear about what alignment feels like. Clear about who reciprocates. Clear about what I refuse to negotiate.

Distance did not weaken me. It strengthened me. Silence did not isolate me. It stabilized me. Boundaries did not harden me. They protected me. And once protection becomes consistent, regression becomes impossible. This was not bitterness. Bitterness revisits. This does not revisit. This is clarity applied.

You did not lose access because I needed space. You lost access because space proved peaceful. Peace is not negotiable once experienced fully. Some people expect endings to perform. To cry. To accuse. To dramatize. But the most permanent endings are quiet. No speech. No spectacle. Just a door that no longer opens. This was never about cutting people off. It was about cutting patterns loose. It was about ending repetition. It was about removing erosion. It was about alignment with the architecture of who I became. I did not unravel to return unchanged. I unraveled to rebuild. I did not set boundaries to debate them. I set them to live by them. I did not choose distance to cause harm. I chose it to preserve peace. This was never about loss. It was about alignment. Alignment does not apologize.

Access was never taken. It was clarified. And what was never aligned was never meant to continue. The door did not slam. It closed. And it did not reopen.

I didn't leave angry.

I didn't leave loudly.

I didn't leave defeated.

I left because staying required me to be smaller than I am.

There is a difference between patience and postponement.

Between loyalty and self-neglect.

Between endurance and alignment.

I learned those differences slowly.

By stretching too far.

By explaining too long.

By staying past expiration.

Growth rarely announces itself.

It accumulates.

It shows up in what you no longer tolerate.

In what you no longer revisit.

In what you no longer negotiate with yourself about.

Some people will read this and feel exposed.

Some will feel relieved.

Some will misunderstand it entirely.

All of that is outside my control.

Clarity does not require consensus.

This was never about cutting people off.

It was about cutting patterns loose.

It was never about isolation.

It was about alignment.

It was never about proving strength.

It was about practicing it.

I do not regret what I carried.

It taught me weight.
I do not regret what I released.
It taught me structure.
I do not regret who fell away.
They taught me standards.
What comes next does not need witnesses.
It does not need validation.
It does not need applause.
It only needs consistency.
The door did not close because I was wounded.
It closed because I was done negotiating with myself.
And once self-negotiation ends,
peace begins.
This is not bitterness.
This is not revenge.
This is not performance.
This is alignment.
And alignment is quiet.
The room is still.
The lesson remains.
Access was never guaranteed.
It was granted.
And now —
it is complete.

EPILOGUE

What Remains

By the time access ended, I was no longer asking who left.

I was asking who I had become.

There is a difference.

Early on, I measured loss by absence.

Who stopped calling.

Who stopped showing up.

Who no longer positioned me at the center of their decisions.

Now I measure differently.

I measure by alignment.

By stability.

By whether my peace requires negotiation.

Access did not disappear from my life.

It narrowed.

It refined.

It became intentional.

The people who remain do not require explanation.
They do not require overextension.
They do not require performance.
They stand.
And so do I.
I no longer confuse intensity with intimacy.
I no longer mistake proximity for loyalty.
I no longer equate endurance with strength.
Strength is restraint.
Strength is consistency.
Strength is the ability to walk away without rehearsing the exit.
There were seasons where I over-functioned.
Where I absorbed imbalance.
Where I kept rooms calm at the expense of myself.
That version of me was not weak.
She was surviving.
But survival is not the same as structure.
Structure does not beg.
It does not argue.
It does not chase clarity from those committed to confusion.
It stands.
If something costs peace, it is too expensive.
If something requires constant explanation, it is misaligned.

If something survives only through your effort, it was never stable.

This is what I learned.

You do not need everyone to understand your shift.

You do not need applause for your discipline.

You do not need permission to close a door that exhausts you.

Completion is quiet.

It does not require a scene.

It requires certainty.

The woman writing these final pages is not the woman who began this story.

She is more measured.

More selective.

More still.

Not colder.

Clearer.

Access was never about who could reach me.

It was about whether I was reachable to myself.

And now, I am.

What remains is not loss.

It is alignment.

And alignment does not negotiate.

— Angela C. Le Blanc

FINAL REFLECTION

Some doors close quietly.
Others close with force.

But sometimes the door closes
because you finally learned
who never deserved access.

Access was never taken from me.
I simply learned who no longer had it.

ACKNOWLEDGMENTS

To my children — Tasha, Kindall, and Keyon —

Tasha, my firstborn daughter, you made me a mother. Through you, I learned responsibility, patience, and the depth of a love that reshaped my life forever.

Kindall, my second-born son, you brought strength and perspective. You reminded me that resilience can be quiet, steady, and deeply grounding.

And Keyon, my last but not least, you arrived as a reminder that joy still finds its way forward. Your presence reinforces hope, laughter, and the courage to keep building.

Each of you holds a distinct place in my life and heart. You are my reason to remain present, to keep growing, and to continue choosing strength. Thank you for walking beside me — knowingly and unknowingly — every step of the way.

George Werner (Deceased)

A great man.

George, you were a man of principle, discipline, and truth. You believed in doing things the right way, even when it was harder, even when it was unpopular. You held standards not to intimidate, but to prepare people for the weight of responsibility.

You believed in me before I fully understood how much that belief would matter. You trusted me with opportunity, with leadership, and with lessons that shaped how I think, how I work, and how I carry myself to this day.

You taught me to be precise.

To be prepared.

To protect my work and my name.

You led with clarity and expected accountability, and because of that, you left people stronger than you found them. I am one of them.

You were not perfect, but you were honest.

You were not gentle, but you were fair.

And you were, without question, a great man.

I am better because I knew you.

Grateful because you invested in me.

And proud to carry forward what you taught.

Thank you, George.

Your legacy lives on.

ABOUT THE AUTHOR

ANGELA C. LE BLANC is a storyteller of power, precision, and reclamation.

She does not write to entertain. She writes to awaken.

Her debut memoir, You Lost Access, marks the beginning of the Access Series — a bold literary movement exploring boundaries, identity, survival, and the moment clarity demands courage.

What began as personal unraveling became strategic rebuilding. What felt like loss became authority.

Angela writes for the woman who has endured in silence. For the woman who rebuilt without applause. For the woman who understands that access is not a privilege granted to others — it is a standard set for herself.

As founder of Le Blanc Ventures LLC, Angela is building more than books. She is building rooms. Experiences. Elevated conversations. The Black Label editions of the Access Series expand the narrative with deeper psychology, sharper truth, and uncompromising power.

Based in Atlanta, Georgia, her work bridges memoir and movement — positioning boundaries not as defense, but as design.

This is not a story about revenge. It is a story about return.

And this is only the beginning.

COMING NEXT IN THE ACCESS SERIES

YOU NEVER HAD ACCESS

You thought the story ended
when the door closed.

It didn't.

That was only separation.
This is evaluation.

In You Lost Access, she walked away.
In You Never Had Access, she understands something
far more dangerous:

Some people were never inside the structure to begin
with.

Love was not the failure.

Alignment was.

Presence was not permission.
Desire was not qualification.

This time, she is not recovering.
She is reinforcing.

Boardrooms will test her.
Proximity will tempt her.

Assumptions will challenge her authority.

Because access is not lost.
It is measured.

And not everyone qualifies.

YOU NEVER HAD ACCESS

Book II – The Access Series